TAKE A CLOSER LOOK AT YOUR
Skin

BY JENNY FRETLAND VANVOORST

Published by The Child's World®
1980 Lookout Drive • Mankato, MN 56003-1705
800-599-READ • www.childsworld.com

Acknowledgments
The Child's World®: Mary Berendes, Publishing Director
Red Line Editorial: Editorial direction and production
The Design Lab: Design
Content Consultant: Jeffrey W. Oseid, MD

Photographs ©: Jason R. Warren/iStockphoto, title;
Shutterstock Images, title, 11, 15, 16, 23; Alex Luengo/
Shutterstock Images , title, 24; Monkey Business Images/
Shutterstock Images, 5; iStockphoto/Thinkstock, 6, 7, 13;
Jupiterimages/Thinkstock, 8; Alila Sao Mai/Shutterstock
Images, 9; N. F. Photography/Shutterstock Images, 17; Steve
Mason/Thinkstock, 18; George Doyle/Thinkstock, 19; Jaimie
Duplass/Shutterstock Images, 20; StockLite/Shutterstock
Images, 21

Front cover: Jason R. Warren/iStockphoto; Alex Luengo/
Shutterstock Images; Shutterstock Images

ISBN 978-1623235543
LCCN 2013931446

Printed in the United States of America
Mankato, MN
July, 2013
PA02175

About the Author

Jenny Fretland VanVoorst is a writer and editor of books for young people. She enjoys learning about all kinds of topics and has written books that range in subject from ancient peoples to artificial intelligence. When she is not reading and writing, Jenny enjoys kayaking, playing the piano, and watching wildlife. She lives in Minneapolis, Minnesota, with her husband, Brian, and their two pets.

Table of Contents

CHAPTER 1

The Skin You're In

Have you ever heard of your birthday suit? This term refers to your skin. It is what you were wearing when you were born. It is funny, but it is true. Your skin is a suit of armor that protects what is inside.

Skin is the largest **organ** in the body. An adult's skin when stretched out is the size of a twin bed sheet! It would weigh as much as an 8-pound (4 kg) house cat. Skin can be thin like the skin on your eyelids. Or it can be thick like the soles of your feet.

Touch is important for human growth. Studies show babies need to be held and cuddled.

Human touch has a powerful effect throughout our lives.

Skin has many important jobs. Skin keeps your insides in your body. It also keeps objects on the outside from going into your body. Skin forms a wall. It keeps water and **germs** away from your internal organs. It also keeps out the cold. Your skin keeps your body warm inside even when it is freezing outside. Your skin also protects your body against overheating by sweating. A healthy body has an internal temperature of 98.6 degrees Fahrenheit (37 degrees Celsius).

Your skin protects your body from extreme heat and cold.

Your skin is also the organ where you can feel the sense of touch. Imagine going to the beach. You feel the crunch of sand between your toes. The sun makes your shoulders warm. And the waves splash on your legs. Because your body is covered with skin, you can feel with all parts of your body. Let's learn more about the skin you're in.

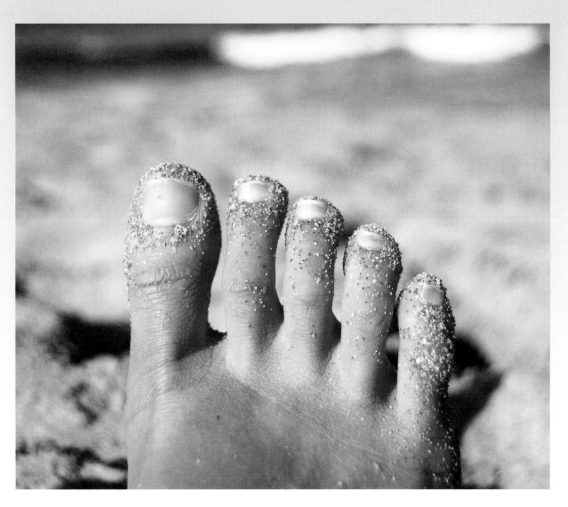

Your skin lets you feel things like sand and water.

CHAPTER 2

Get Under Your Skin

Take a look in the mirror. Does your skin look healthy and bright? Think again. Everything you see is dead skin.

The top layer of skin might look healthy, but it is made up of dead skin cells.

The top layer of your skin is made of dead skin cells. This thin layer is called the **epidermis**. New skin cells form at the bottom of the epidermis. Then they move upward. As skin cells die, they are pushed together and flattened. This is the skin you see. These dead skin cells overlap like shingles on a roof. They form a protective wall for the tissues beneath. You are always shedding these dead skin cells. In one minute you may lose up to 40,000 skin cells!

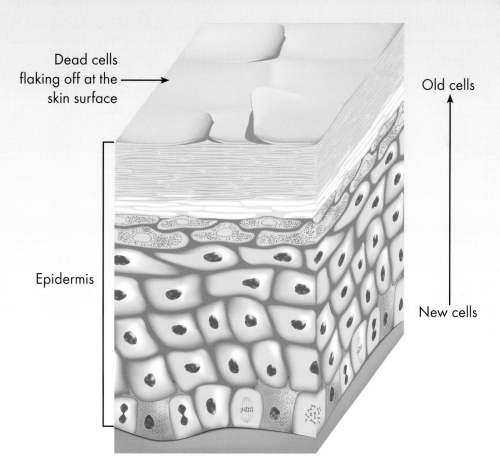

Dead cells flaking off at the skin surface

Old cells

Epidermis

New cells

A skin cell lives for about 35 days. The cell is created and sheds in this time. In one year you will have shed more than 12 sets of skin!

The epidermis is covered in an oily coating. This coating is like a raincoat. It keeps water from going into the body. But this raincoat is not completely waterproof. Your skin will absorb some water. Do you like to go swimming? Are your fingers and toes wrinkly afterward? That is what happens when your skin absorbs water.

The epidermis is very thin like a page in a book. Underneath the epidermis is a thicker layer called the **dermis**. The dermis houses blood vessels, sweat **glands**, and nerve endings. Blood vessels help your skin keep an even temperature. They increase or decrease blood flow to the surface of the skin. Sweat glands cool the skin by releasing sweat.

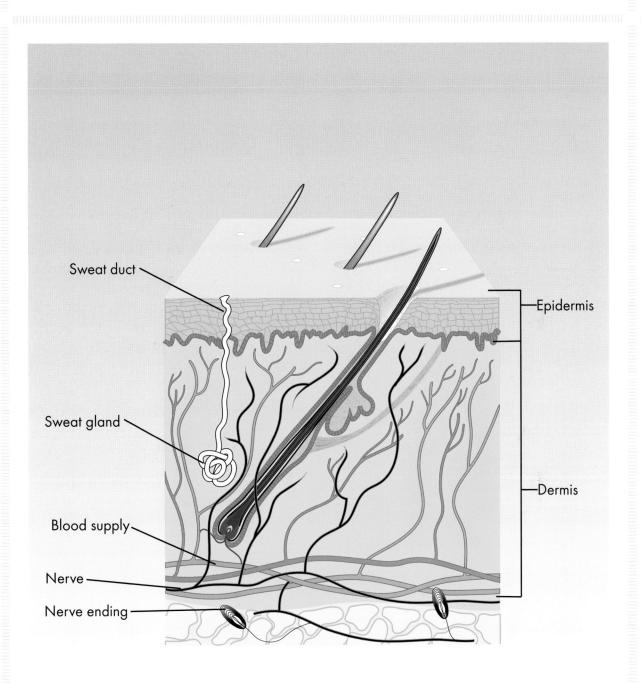

Sweat duct

Sweat gland

Blood supply

Nerve

Nerve ending

Epidermis

Dermis

The nerve endings give you the sense of touch. The nerves end in sensors that work together. The sensors detect texture, pressure, movement, temperature, itchiness, and pain. A million sensors fit in an area the size of your fingernail. When you burn yourself, these sensors detect both heat and pain. They send a message through the nerves to the brain. The brain decodes the message. It sends your muscles a message to move away from the source of the pain. Nerve cells allow you to feel a painful burn. But they also allow you to feel a cat's soft fur.

Fingertips have more nerve endings than anywhere else on the body.

The nerves in your skin will tell your brain when something is hot.

CHAPTER 3

When Good Skin Goes Bad

Your skin works hard to protect you. But sometimes skin hurts or gets cut. Pain is the first sign something is wrong. Pain is a signal that cells have been damaged. Do not ignore this signal. You might hurt your skin more. Delaying care might also make a wound harder to heal.

Cuts and scrapes are common injuries. You might get a cut from a sharp knife. You might also scrape your knee on the sidewalk. Your amazing skin will heal itself over time. Skin cells multiply and rush to seal up the wound. Most cuts and scrapes do not go deeper than the epidermis. They can be cleaned and covered with a bandage. If the cut is very large or deep, you may need stitches. A doctor will fix your skin like you might fix a torn shirt.

Scar tissue is made of stronger material than regular skin. Scarred skin is stronger than it was before it was injured.

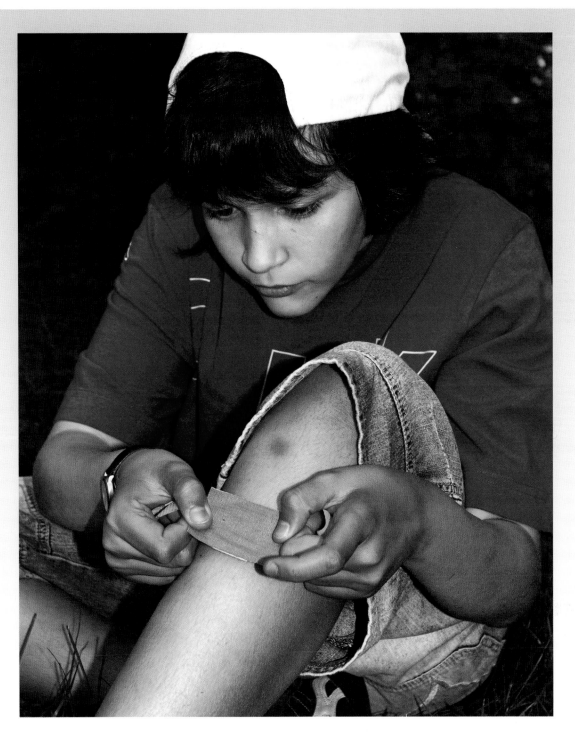

When you get a cut or scrape, you can protect it with a bandage.

Sunburn is also a common problem. Skin burns if it is in the sun too long. It becomes red and sore. Sometimes it peels. Once again, your amazing skin works to protect itself. **Melanin** is a substance your skin makes to protect itself. This substance protects your skin from the sun's damaging rays. Melanin causes your skin to tan. Darker skin has more melanin than lighter skin. Sometimes the sun burns before enough melanin can be made. You get sunburn. A sunburn does not just hurt. It can damage your skin and lead to more serious problems.

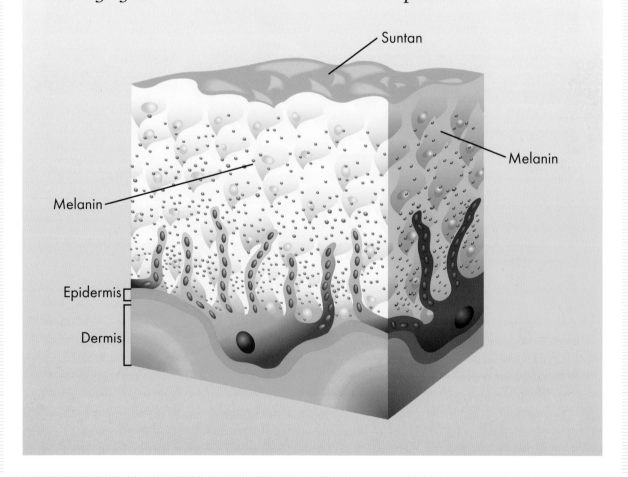

Suntan

Melanin

Melanin

Epidermis

Dermis

Have you ever touched a plant like poison ivy? You probably ended up with red, blistering, and itchy skin. The plant's sap irritates the skin and causes a rash. Scented laundry detergent can cause some people's skin to itch. Certain drugs can have an effect on your skin, too. Steer clear of things you know will irritate you. Your skin will thank you for it.

Certain plants might cause a skin rash.

CHAPTER 4

Skin Deep

Your skin does a good job of taking care of itself. There are some things you can do to help make its work easier.

Keep your skin clean. It comes in contact with dirt and germs during the day. Wash it with soap and water. Then pat it dry rather than rubbing.

Washing your hands keeps your skin clean.

Treat cuts and scrapes gently. Clean the wound and cover it with an **antibiotic** cream. Then cover it with a bandage to protect it. Do not pick scabs. They are part of the healing process.

People in many cultures decorate their skin as a way to express themselves. Makeup, tattoos, and piercings are some of the more common methods.

To avoid sunburn, wear sunscreen when you are outside. You can get sunburn even when it is cloudy. Choose a sunscreen with an **SPF** of 30 or higher. Apply it evenly over all exposed areas. Make sure to reapply sunscreen after swimming or sweating heavily. Or avoid the sun during its brightest times—between 10 a.m. and 2 p.m.

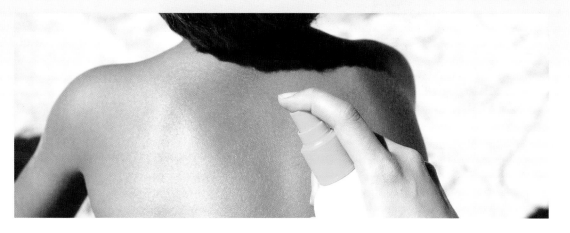

It is important to wear sunscreen when you're outside.

You can also treat your skin well from the inside. Drink plenty of water. Eat healthy foods. A balanced diet will give your skin energy to do its job. Make sure to get plenty of rest. Much of your skin's repair work happens while you sleep. Eight hours a night is the right amount for most people.

Your skin renews itself while you sleep.

Your skin lets you touch and feel the world around you.

There is only one organ that lets you feel touch. Thanks to skin you can feel a soft blanket or the rough bark on a tree. Your skin is the largest part of you. Take care of the skin you are in.

antibiotic (an-ti-bye-OT-ik) An antibiotic is a drug used to cure infections and diseases. If you get a cut, clean it with antibiotic cream.

dermis (DER-mis) The dermis is an inner layer of living skin cells that contains nerves, glands, and blood vessels. The dermis is a thicker layer of skin.

epidermis (ep-uh-DER-mis) The epidermis is the thin outer layer of skin. Dead skin cells make up the epidermis.

germs (JURMS) Germs are very small living things that can cause disease. Skin keeps germs from entering the body.

glands (GLANDS) Glands are organs that allow substances to leave the body. The sweat glands allow sweat to leave the body.

melanin (MEL-uhn-in) Melanin is a substance in skin that protects it from light. Melanin helps skin to tan.

organ (OR-guhn) An organ is a part of the body that does a particular job. The skin is the largest organ in the body.

SPF (SPF) SPF stands for sun protection factor. Sunscreen with an SPF of 30 or higher is a good choice.

LEARN MORE

BOOKS

Parker, Steve. *The Senses*. Chicago: Raintree, 2004.

Parker, Steve. *Skin, Muscles, and Bones*. Milwaukee: Gareth Stevens, 2004.

WEB SITES

Visit our Web site for links about the skin: **childsworld.com/links**

Note to Parents, Teachers, and Librarians: We routinely verify our Web links to make sure they are safe and active sites. So encourage your readers to check them out!

INDEX

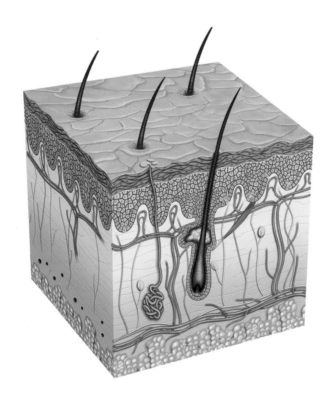